# CRIME AND PUZZLEMENT

## My Cousin Phoebe

# CRIME AND Puzzlement

## MY COUSIN PHOEBE

**24** SOLVE-THEM-YOURSELF PICTURE MYSTERIES

## Lawrence Treat

### ILLUSTRATED BY DEAN BORNSTEIN

AN OWL BOOK · HENRY HOLT AND COMPANY

NEW YORK

Henry Holt and Company, Inc.
*Publishers since 1866*
115 West 18th Street
New York, New York 10011

Henry Holt® is a registered trademark
of Henry Holt and Company, Inc.

Published in Canada by Fitzhenry & Whiteside Limited,
91 Granton Drive, Richmond Hill, Ontario L4B 2N5.

Library of Congress Cataloging-in-Publication Data
Treat, Lawrence.
Crime and puzzlement, my cousin Phoebe :
24 solve-them-yourself picture mysteries / by Lawrence
Treat; illustrated by Dean Bornstein. — 1st ed.
p.     cm.
"An Owl book."
1. Puzzles.     2. Detective and mystery stories.
3. Picture puzzles.     I. Title.     II. Title: Crime
and puzzlement.     III. Title: My cousin Phoebe.
GV1507.D4T7345   1991                 91-21191
                                        CIP

ISBN 0-8050-1592-2

Henry Holt books are available for special
promotions and premiums. For details contact:
Director, Special Markets.

First Edition—1991

Printed in the United States of America
All first editions are printed on acid-free paper.∞

10   9   8   7   6   5   4   3   2

Illustration for "At the Professional Level" and riddle on page vii
reprinted by permission of Clark Boardman Company, Ltd.

# CONTENTS

Introduction   vii

How to Solve the Puzzles   ix


A Tale of Hate   1

Board to Death   3

A Pair of Roos   5

The Fair Evangeline   7

Whiz Kid   9

Witness, the Cat   11

Involving the Rear End   13

Play On, Oh Lovely Music   15

Without Mirrors, Please   17

Tale of a Tub   19

Spitfire   21

All Around the Maypole   23

Ex Libris   25

A Matter of Gravity   27

By Appointment Only   29

The End of Euphoria   31

The Three Graces   33

The Vandals   35

57th Heaven   37

Bombs in Toyland   39

The Three Wise Men   41

At the Professional Level   43

Fido, Rover, and Spot   45

The March of the Marchioness   47


Solutions   49

# INTRODUCTION

$S$hortly after Justice Oliver Wendell Holmes retired from the U.S. Supreme Court, then in his eighties, a friend of his dropped by and found him studying classical Greek grammar.

"Why study Greek, at your age?" the friend asked.

Holmes bristled, but stated what to him was obvious. "Why, sir," he said, "I wish to improve my mind."

Tackling these puzzles is not guaranteed to improve yours, but it just might, and it certainly should amuse you.

For instance, aren't you dying to know why the marchioness of Secks-Ruma had to rush out to her hairdresser? Or why Salvina Odium should never have opened that closet door? And who won that strip poker game that caught the art world with its pants down?

This book is designed specifically for the age group of eight to eighty, although there are precocious specimens at either end of the spectrum. People put these puzzles to all sorts of uses: A training program for detectives uses them, teachers calm down their fidgety pupils by administering a puzzle or two, and schools have made them part of a curriculum to teach observation and logic. Foreigners studying English become so absorbed in these puzzles that they end up speaking as fluently as Americans—or so their tutors tell me. But you don't have to study a new language to be lured by these puzzles. Ordinary curiosity will do it.

You will meet all kinds of perpetrators in these pages, some of them shoddy and others as chic as the Three Graces, who committed murder in full view of a dozen people, and got away with it.

The detectives I've come across over the years are of varied abilities, although nobody reaches the stature of my Cousin Phoebe. Frankly, she's not my cousin, she's my aunt. But she always loved strong language and, as a result, she was known as that cussin' Phoebe. Somehow or other I got my zees and my esses mixed up and called her my Cousin Phoebe, and the name stuck. I'm told that even as a child she had an unusual, investigative talent, and some of her earliest cases are presented in this book. To see if you can match her professional caliber, test yourself by reading the sentence in the following box.

> FINISHED FILES ARE THE RESULT OF
> YEARS OF SCIENTIFIC STUDY
> COMBINED WITH THE EXPERIENCE
> OF YEARS.

Next, count the number of F's in that sentence. Count them only once. Record your findings and refer to page 49 for the correct answer.

There is no morality and no justice in this book, except what you yourself inject into it. There are victims as pure and innocent as the Fair Evangeline, and as loathsome as Hector and Salvina Odium. Most of the killings are pretty ordinary stuff—a knife or a gun or a solid, blunt instrument—but there are a few on the esoteric side, like the use of akrokanthera. How do you administer such a thing? Or for that matter, pronounce it?

This book is designed equally for the keen-minded who like a challenge, and for the lazy sort who are free to look up the answers in the back and tell themselves they could have solved the case all along. And to them I say, why not? For those who have read thus far, there's nothing but pleasure ahead, with or without a pencil. Or a pen. That's optional.

# HOW TO SOLVE THE PUZZLES

1. Always read the narrative first. It supplies you with vital clues.

2. Read all the questions through without trying to answer them. This will give you a sense of what to look for in the picture.

3. Examine the picture.

4. Grab your pencil.

5. Answer the questions, one at a time and in order. If you're a beginner, it might help if you check your answers as you go along to make sure that you're on the right track. Once you think your detecting skills are sharp enough, you may want to skip the preliminary questions altogether and go straight for the big one at the end.

6. Look at the solution and either congratulate yourself on a job well done or resolve to do better next time. Then move on to the next puzzle.

# CRIME AND PUZZLEMENT

## My Cousin Phoebe

# A TALE OF HATE

Dear Sal,
It's now 2 p.m. and your new dress just came in and so I hung it up. Had to leave in a rush. Back Thursday.

Hector

The Odiums, Hector and Salvina, hated each other from the day they'd met, and married out of sheer spite. Once wedded, their hate burgeoned and they swore to kill each other. To make the prospective murder financially worthwhile, they insured each other for $500,000, with the survivor as beneficiary, which stabilized the marriage and kept it going on a mutually dissatisfactory basis.

Robin Bedfellow, a wandering minstrel, knew nothing of the Odiums' feud one early morning when his car broke down in a desert area near San Diego. He walked to the nearest house in the hope of getting help. Since the door of the Odium residence was unlocked, he opened it and went in, and was shocked to see what you see here.

What conclusions do you think he reached, and what should he have done about it?

## Questions

1. Are rattlesnakes unusual in this area?

2. Was Salvina aware of the danger of snakes?

3. Do rattlesnakes usually make unprovoked attacks?

4. Is the room neat?

5. Did Salvina get home after dark?

6. Do you think the closet door was open when Salvina came home?

7. How do you think the snake got in the house?

8. Where do you think the snake was when Salvina entered the room?

9. Why do you think Salvina fell?

10. Can you reconstruct the sequence of events that led to Salvina's fall?

*Solution on page 49.*

# BOARD TO DEATH

The Robe and Disrobe Company ("Something for Everybody") of Omaha, Nebraska, was holding its annual directors' meeting. At the top of the agenda was a bitterly contested proposal to coat its products with a secret aphrodisiac, which several of the directors used regularly. A tie vote was expected among the executives, after which Willy Wiggle-Waggle, chairman of the board, would cast the deciding ballot. It was rumored that he favored applying the aphrodisiac to pajamas and nightgowns only, a compromise that enraged both sides of the controversy.

Wiggle-Waggle had just called for a vote on the issue when suddenly the lights went out, apparently due to a short circuit. Nobody could see what happened immediately afterwards, but somehow or other Hopalong Hopson left the room, found the circuit box, and restored the lights. By then, everybody had left his seat and the scene was as you see it here. Obviously, no further proposals were considered that day.

As was the custom of the company, the directors were seated alphabetically around the table. Moving counterclockwise from the left, they were: Bully Bison, Cappy Capstan, Dodo Dodson, Wiggle-Waggle, Funny Fonson, Goodie Gotson, and Hopson.

Who killed Wiggle-Waggle?

## Questions

1. Was the aphrodisiac motion the first order of business?

2. Was Wiggle-Waggle given a hard blow?

3. Do you think the murder was planned?

4. Do you think the killer had an accomplice?

5. Did the killer have to act quickly?

6. Who was in the best position to kill Wiggle-Waggle?

7. Who killed Wiggle-Waggle?

*Solution on page 50.*

# A PAIR OF ROOS

Daniel Micklemouse was having a brandy and soda in the Northwest Orient first-class lounge when a hoary stranger sat down next to him and said, "Hark unto me, O traveler."

Micklemouse said, "I'm harking."

"Well and good," the hoary stranger said. "Suppose two kangaroos, opposite each other and each of them exactly two hundred yards away from a tray of succulent vegetables, start out for the tray at precisely the same instant. Each of them makes exactly ten yards per leap. If atmospheric conditions and all other elements are identical, the only difference being that the kangaroo named Joseph travels from east to west, while the kangaroo named Josephine goes from west to east, who gets to the vegetables first?"

Micklemouse thought for a moment before asking, "Which way does the earth rotate?"

"West to east," the hoary stranger said promptly.

Micklemouse took another swig of brandy before speaking. "The problem intrigues me," he said, "but I'm on my way to a wedding in Australia and my plane leaves shortly. I think I'd better go watch some kangaroos before answering your question. Would you mind waiting?"

"How long?" the stranger asked.

"Eighteen days."

"Fair enough. Here?"

"At this very spot."

Micklemouse went to Australia, attended the wedding, and fell in love with one of the bridesmaids, who accompanied him while he made an intensive study of kangaroos. She was still with him when he returned to the lounge on the eighteenth day and found the hoary stranger waiting for Micklemouse's answer.

What was it?

*Solution on page 50.*

# THE FAIR EVANGELINE

The Admirable Farragut was not only a talented painter, but one of the fastest who ever lived: He could complete a portrait in five minutes. His all-time record was a landscape done in 2 minutes and $36^{11}/_{100}$ seconds.

In fact, his only shortcoming was that his amours went almost as fast as his brush, often with disastrous results. But no other tragedy approached that of the Fair Evangeline, whose body was found in a shallow grave one moonlit night.

"I expected to meet her at a ruined house on the shores of Lake Rembrandt," the Admirable Farragut told my Cousin Phoebe, to whom he tried to sell the painting which is reproduced here. "Unfortunately," he said, "she never arrived, but while waiting, I painted this landscape exactly the way I saw it, including a figure a mile away from me and highlighted by the moonlight reflected from the lake. After I'd finished, I picked up my field glasses and focused on the figure, which I could then see clearly. He was digging a grave, and to my surprise I recognized him. He was—but his name escapes me at the moment, except that it's the same last name as his wife's, the Fair Evangeline, whose last name is— Good Grief! She never told me!"

The husband in question, C. Starrs, was an astronomer of note. He told my Cousin Phoebe he'd been wandering around Lake Rembrandt in the hope of sighting a new comet. When the police questioned him, Starrs said, "I saw the man who was digging the grave, and I recognized him as the Admirable Farragut."

After that, Starrs refused to speak, except to make a brief statement. "The Admirable Farragut," he said, "is a lousy painter."

My Cousin Phoebe agreed, but didn't press the matter. Instead, she pointed out that the case hinged on proving which of the two men was a liar, of which there was no doubt.

Whom did she accuse, and why?

---

## Questions

1. Is there any evidence to support the Admirable Farragut's statement?

2. Is there any evidence to support C. Starr's statement?

3. Does the painting itself contain any evidence indicating the time when the grave digger was at work?

4. Did the Admirable Farragut have a possible motive?

5. Did C. Starrs have a possible motive?

6. Where was Farragut standing when he painted the picture?

7. Who killed the Fair Evangeline?

*Solution on page 51.*

# WHIZ KID

Sally Forth was a bright little girl who had always hoped she'd get kidnapped so she could escape and capture her captors, but that was when she was only five years old. When she was seven, she was older and wiser, and realized she'd never be able to capture anybody. Nevertheless, just in case, she made plans to leave at least a few clues to her whereabouts.

When it did actually happen, the kidnappers phoned her parents and demanded $50,000. To convince them that they were really holding Sally, they let her speak to her parents. She sounded innocent enough when she said she was all right; she was being well treated and had only one complaint.

"They want fifty thousand," she said, "but I'm worth a lot more. At least a million."

"Where are you?" Mr. Forth asked, hoping she'd manage to tell.

"They'll kill me if I tell you," she said, "but you can phone me at—" At that point a voice broke in and the connection was cut.

Mr. Forth immediately notified the police, who went to work on tracing the call. Eventually they narrowed it down to a few houses and then to the one where Sally had been held temporarily. Searching for evidence, they found this bit of paper in a garbage pail. From Sally's phone conversation with her parent ("You can phone me at—"), the police reasoned that she knew where she was to be taken and had left this scrap of paper as a clue.

The police realized at once that this was a fictitious phone number, because the second digit of all area codes is either a one or a zero. They then proceeded to decipher the code.

Can you?

---

## Questions

1. Did Sally know where the kidnappers were taking her?

2. Did Sally write this note?

3. Do you think the numerals were an attempt to convey a message?

4. Do you think the kidnappers found Sally's scribblings and thought them of no importance?

5. Would the kidnappers probably check up on what might appear to be a phone number?

6. What was the key to the code that Sally was using?

7. What was Sally's message?

*Solution on page 51.*

# WITNESS, THE CAT

$A$t 5 P.M. Dixie Tittlemouse, club stewardess at the Sappy Mill Country Club, knocked on the door of the Bon-kei* room. Alarmed when nobody answered, she banged away until Ulrica van Stamen finally staggered over, slid back the bolt, and managed to drag open the door. Upon entering the room, Dixie saw what you see in the sketch. She immediately noticed the empty frame and exclaimed (she was French), "Ah, pauvre Pierre Auguste!"

Unfortunately, the only witness, dead or alive, as to who had stolen the missing Renoir, was Dilly the cat—a club favorite because its meow was a perfect C major, and it could walk along the top of a tennis net without falling. The painting had been appraised at $2 million.

Dixie had some difficulty in waking Ulrica's companions, who were seated counter-clockwise from the right: Anthony Adipose, Vera Cruse, and Felonius Winkleman. All four were club members and experienced poker players. But they had known each other only slightly before they'd sat down at the card table. They played for moderate stakes and were comfortably pickled in alcohol when Felonius suggested strip poker. Ulrica exclaimed, "Wow! I hope I lose!" Vera checked a couple of her zippers, and Anthony leered at the two women and said, "My deal." In due course, all four admitted that they'd passed out and consequently could contribute nothing relevant to the theft of the Renoir.

Later on, after a diligent search, the police admitted that they were unable to locate the painting. My Cousin Phoebe, who happened to have stopped at the club for a few rounds of golf after school, knew better and reconstructed the crime. Can you?

*Bon-kei is the Japanese art of miniature landscape using tiny props.

## Questions

1. Were all four people apparently drunk?

2. Was the painting hidden in the room, and if so, where?

3. Could a drunken person have cut the picture from its frame?

4. Could a fifth person have entered the room during the night without the knowledge of any of the poker players?

5. Did the cat either eat, drink, or go to the bathroom at the bon-kei?

6. Why do you think the cat fell?

7. Who stole the Renoir?

*Solution on page 52.*

# INVOLVING THE REAR END

That Nutty Fregosa, a well-known kite flyer, got nipped in the left buttock, thus suffering pain, humiliation, and a substantial medical bill, was admitted by both sides of the case of *Fregosa v. Sykes*. The question was whether Bill Sykes's hundred-pound Alsatian, Numismatic, had or had not acted on orders.

Sykes, a methodical man, claimed (1) he wasn't within sight of Nutty and therefore could not have taken action against him; (2) Numismatic had acted on his own initiative and on the basis of his educated olfaction; (3) the episode had been generated by a trespass on the part of the plaintiff; and (4) Numismatic, although a gourmet, loved children and had never taken a bite out of a child under the age of eight, despite the fact that such tender flesh would make a far more succulent tidbit than the stringy, desiccated meat of the plaintiff's sinistral, ischial tuberosity.

Nutty claimed he had not been trespassing and that even if he had been, he'd been pursuing the peaceable sport of kite flying. The dog had come upon him with malice aforethought, having been sicced on him by Sykes with whom he, Nutty Fregosa, had had an unfortunate past confrontation.

By sheer chance Sissy Atkins had been photographing the area ("It's so beautiful, I almost fainted"), and a replica of one of her pictures taken moments before Numismatic's charge is reproduced here.

In an act of pure altruism Sissy offered the picture to Nutty, who said "Ah!" and in his exuberance kissed her on the lips, obliquely but expertly. Sissy almost swooned, but managed to steady herself by grabbing hold of Nutty.

The photograph was the only piece of evidence that Nutty offered. The judge listened to the opening statements of both attorneys, then appeared to doze off, but woke up at the end of the trial and almost immediately granted a motion for a directed verdict. Did he rule in favor of Nutty, the plaintiff, or Sykes, the defendant, and why?

---

# Questions

1. Was Nutty trespassing?

2. Was he on a peaceful expedition?

3. Does a kite flyer have the right to trespass?

4. Is it credible that a dog would attack a trespasser on its own initiative?

5. Did the dog scent Nutty and attack on his own?

6. Was Nutty within sight of the distant figure?

7. Against whom did the judge direct the verdict?

*Solution on page 53.*

# PLAY ON, OH LOVELY MUSIC

Gaston Quirkenbocker was a superb violinist. He had organized the Quirkenbocker Quartet and made it famous. He was the glue that held it together and gave it balance and fervor and coherence. Nevertheless, his colleagues feared and hated him.

This was so because he had a violent temper and had once reportedly broken the hand of a talented pianist who'd had the nerve to criticize him. But the musicians suppressed their feelings and never dared to say or do anything overt.

Some say Ulric von Tramm, the violist, hated him most, but Ignatz Smith, the cellist, disagreed. "I think Evelina (Evelina Forceps, the pianist) hated him more. Women have deeper feelings." But their personal animosity was of no concern to Quirkenbocker himself.

"People hate me," he said, "because they envy me. Even little Paige Turner, who turns the pages for Evelina, would like to kill me, so let them snivel." And with that, he twirled his mustache, which he redesigned every two months.

One recent Sunday evening during a particularly sumptuous concert, at the moment depicted in the sketch, Quirkenbocker suddenly went livid and stopped the performance cold. He turned to the audience and accused his colleagues of a plot to sabotage him; he gave each of them in turn a vicious slap, and walked off the platform.

In the ensuing argument backstage, Quirkenbocker was shot and killed. His three colleagues were charged with murder and conspiracy to commit a murder. They were subsequently convicted and sentenced to ten years each in prison.

By examining the picture, can you decide who was responsible for the trick that was the underlying cause of the crime?

## Questions

1. Who had an opportunity to tamper with Gaston's score?

2. Whose picture did Quirkenbocker find when he turned the page of his score?

3. Did the other members of the Quirkenbocker Quartet find anything unusual when they turned their pages?

4. Why did Gaston stop the performance?

5. Who do you think tampered with Gaston's score?

*Solution on page 53.*

# WITHOUT MIRRORS, PLEASE

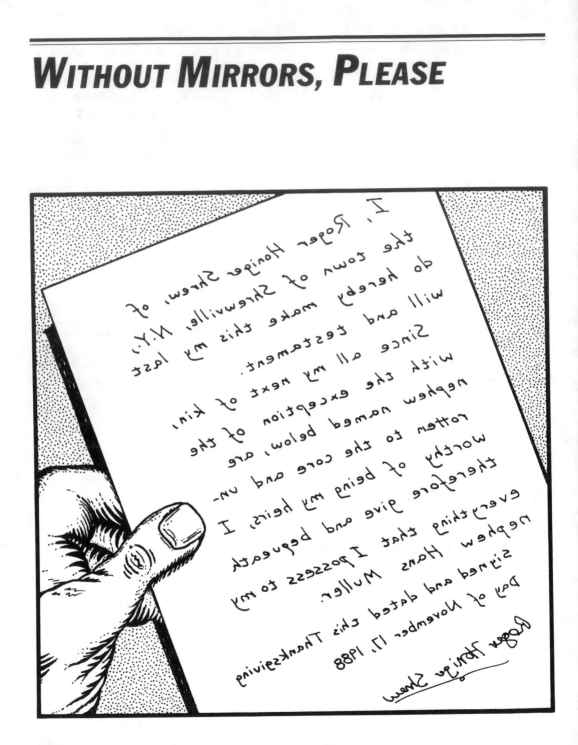

$R$oger Honiger was a wealthy and eccentric bachelor who had three nephews whom he invited for dinner on the first and fifteenth of every month. He gloried in tantalizing them by telling them he intended to make one of them his sole heir, but wouldn't make up his mind until after they'd left for the evening.

They came to his house unwillingly, aware of the consequences of a refusal, and among themselves they discussed what they called the Roger Honiger Sweepstakes.

In the course of time, Roger did what everybody had been hoping he'd do—he died. His three nephews, namely Vladimir, Sean, and Antonio, attended the funeral dutifully, and waited for the executor to go through a host of documents piled in drawers, desks, and on closet shelves. In due time, he came up with a large number of holographic wills (that is, wills written entirely in the testator's handwriting, and requiring no witnesses). The three latest of these wills were dated April 1, 1987, and each one designated a different nephew as sole heir.

And then the Berlin Wall came tumbling down.

Enter Hans, the forgotten nephew from East Germany. Hans, who spoke excellent English, settled temporarily in Roger's house and went about examining it. In the course of rummaging around, he found, or claimed to have found, a copy of a will dated November 17, 1988, somehow wedged in a side compartment of Roger's big rolltop desk. The handwriting of the will apparently matched that of the April Fool's Day wills, but named Hans as the sole legal heir.

Assuming that, if the original of a document cannot be found, a carbon copy is as valid as the original would have been, do you think that the Thanksgiving Day will (reproduced here) is valid as a holograph?

---

## Questions

1. Decipher and transcribe the will, *and use no mirrors!*

2. Do you think that the April Fool's Day wills are invalid because they are obviously a joke?

3. How do you think this carbon copy came about?

4. Do you think the November 17 document is invalid, and if so why?

*Solution on page 54.*

# TALE OF A TUB

$A$s is well known, Napoleon planned his military strategy while soaking in a hot bath on the night before a battle. Several tubs have been identified as his think tanks, such as the tub in which he bathed in camp on the eve of the battle of Waterloo. Josephine Boharr presumably owned it, but offered it for sale when she found herself in financial straits. Newly painted a sparkling white, the tub was auctioned off amid considerable excitement, since the main bidders were the notorious collectors Alphonso O'Shaughnessy of Brazil and Roland LeBras of Toulouse. Because Alphonso was far wealthier than Roland, it was a forgone conclusion that Alphonso would be the winner, and at $50,000 Roland dropped out. With characteristic Gallic suavity, Roland congratulated Alphonso and wished him many happy baths, as hot as possible.

My Cousin Phoebe had heard of the exchange and, like most people, thought it amusing but harmless. That is, until someone knifed and killed Alphonso while he was reclining in his newly acquired tub.

Alphonso's valet, Marshal Nay, told the police that on the evening of Alphonso's death he had had two visitors—Roland LeBras and Josephine Boharr. It followed that whichever of the two had been the last visitor had to be the murderer, but naturally each of them denied that honor, although both admitted to having visited Alphonso. Marshal, however, was unable to remember who had come first. "Too much brandy," he said, "and at best, my memory is fuzzy."

My Cousin Phoebe loved the idea of a drunken valet too finicky to point out a murderer, but when consulted, she asked two or three questions pertaining to the evidence given by the first police officer on the scene, whose testimony is approximated in the sketch herewith. On the basis of the sketch and the facts given above, what is your conclusion?

## Questions

1. Could a tall man fit into the tub?

2. Was Napoleon short?

3. Did Roland have a motive for killing Alphonso?

4. Do you think Alphonso was gypped?

5. Did Josephine have a motive?

6. Do you think that Alphonso would have let a woman come into the bathroom while he was relaxing in the tub?

7. Was there a struggle?

8. Who killed Alphonso of Brazil?

*Solution on page 54.*

# SPITFIRE

Because Jesse Varlet was a spitfire and everybody knew it, Police Chief Felicity Keene stopped by occasionally to see Jesse to find out what she was up to. But one Wednesday afternoon Felicity found her strangled and lying next to her kitchen counter, as shown.

Felicity realized at once that there were three suspects. The first was Jesse's estranged husband, Nicholas, whom she was divorcing. The second was her neighbor, Angel Blackhead, the only honest-to-goodness gangster in all of West Copernicus, and with whom she was feuding over her right to use a shortcut which traversed a corner of his property. The third was Sweet William, a neighborhood handyman, big in muscle and small in brainpower, who mowed lawns and had made passes at Jesse in the past. She had sworn to a friend that she'd never go near "that big dumb oaf."

None of the three had a credible alibi. Sweet William claimed he'd gone into the house for a drink of water, seen the body, and then panicked and ran away lest he be accused. Both Nick and Angel said they'd never been near the house, but refused to elaborate.

Felicity did all the right things, such as calling in the medical examiner and the state Bureau of Investigation, after which she sat down and examined the evidence and reached her own conclusion.

What was it, and what was her reasoning?

---

## Questions

1. Do the wine and glasses indicate a friendly meeting?

2. Did Sweet William leave the lawn without finishing his job?

3. Is it likely that Jesse sat down with Sweet William for a friendly drink?

4. Is it likely that she had a friendly drink with Nick?

5. Which of the three suspects would have jimmied open the cabinet door in order to have a drink with Jesse?

6. Do you think that Nick had an 11 A.M. appointment with Jesse?

7. Do you think that Jesse had a drink with either Sweet William or Angel?

8. Who killed Jesse?

*Solution on page 55.*

# ALL AROUND THE MAYPOLE

In a remote mountain village where age-old customs are still observed, it was a traditional May Day rite for six spotless damsels to dance around the maypole. And this, my Cousin Phoebe had to see.

Unnoticed among the spectators, she watched, and was fascinated by two large dogs (Bub and Tub) who sat directly in front of her. Both were intent on the dancing, but after a few minutes and for no apparent reason, Bub suddenly sprang into action. Afterwards he ran off, with Tub in hot pursuit. At the assault, the six spotless damsels fell down in a heap, but only five got up. Cherie, the sixth, had been fatally stabbed.

When the crowd became aware of the tragedy, some of them became hysterical as they rushed out to the maypole, but my Cousin Phoebe—with the scene you see engraved sharply in her mind—remained where she was. Later, she learned that the names of the six, each of whom had her initials on her garland, were Amore, Belinda, Cherie, Dearie, Ecstata, and Fair.

On the basis of the sketch, and what you've been told above, my Cousin Phoebe was able to point out who killed Cherie. Can you?

---

## Questions

1. Do you think one of the dancers killed Cherie?

2. Was it easy to conceal the knife?

3. Do you think that any of the damsels would be a reliable witness to the stabbing?

4. Do you think that Bub attacked on signal?

5. If your answer to (4) is yes, who do you think gave the signal?
   (a) A bystander.
   (b) One of the dancers.

6. Was the homicide premeditated?

7. Who was in the best position to signal Bub?

8. Who killed Cherie?

*Solution on page 56.*

# Ex Libris

When the sacred silence of the Abelaro Municipal Library was broken by the loud ringing of a bell and someone shouting "Fire!" Miss Goody Quicksilver, the librarian, kept her head and controlled any potential panic. As it turned out, the incident was caused by an ordinary, spring-wound alarm clock. It was still ringing when the Rinkle brothers, distinguished twin historians, raced to the scene and discovered the body of their colleague, Miguel Pinchnose, lying on the floor. He had been shot and the gun lay nearby.

Goody, known as a model librarian who knew almost every book in the library, was also able to identify the victim. She explained that he was a well-known scholar who had recently resigned as the editor of the *Anglo-Saxon Quarterly* in order to write a book on the Venerable Bede. Shaking with righteous anger, she vowed to bring to justice the miscreant who had committed this dastardly crime.

The police were less emotional. They surveyed the scene, took photographs, dusted for fingerprints, and questioned everyone who had been in the library. Several persons had noticed Pinchnose walk past them and go toward the rare book section, but no one had noticed anyone else in the area. Then, by sheer luck, they found the janitor, Sammy Skitch, hiding in a broom closet. After admitting that the alarm clock was his but claiming it had been stolen a few days ago from its place in the broom closet, he said he'd heard it ring and recognized its tinny tone as his. Because he was afraid he'd be blamed for the incident and lose his job, he hid in the closet until the police found him.

The main problem in charging Sammy with the murder of Pinchnose was the lack of motive. At this point, my Cousin Phoebe, who happened to be in the building in order to give a lecture on prehistoric mating techniques, sized up the situation, asked a few questions, and gave the police their case.

What did Phoebe see, what did she figure out, and what did she tell the police?

---

## Questions

1. Had there been a struggle?

2. What was probably the purpose of the alarm clock?

3. Were Pinchnose's notes stolen?

4. What was the motive for the crime?

5. Do you think Sammy was interested in stealing Pinchnose's notebook notes?

6. Do you believe Sammy's statement that his clock was stolen?

7. Who had an opportunity to take Sammy's alarm clock?

8. Who killed Pinchnose?

*Solution on page 57.*

# A Matter of Gravity

Everybody hates a kid who's not only smarter than he or she is, but rubs it in. Thus, the only reason my Cousin Phoebe condescended to go to Theophrastus Stichmeyer's eleventh birthday party was in the hope that Theo would burn his fingers on the Roman candles to be set off in the Stichmeyer backyard.

Theo didn't. Not only that, but he exposed my Cousin Phoebe to a series of grueling questions that left her hanging on the ropes and wishing she'd paid more attention to that fifth-grade science course.

## Questions

1. "Phoebe," Theo said, looking as innocent as a Botticelli cherub, "if you were shipping a bale of polar bear furs from the North Pole to Belem, would the bale have the same weight at both weighing stations?"

   "I wouldn't ship them to Belem," said my Cousin Phoebe, who was a whiz at geography. "What would they do with furs, there on the equator? Unless you mean Belem, Portugal, and even there you wouldn't have much of a market."

   "But if," Theo said, thinking he had her trapped. "*If* you did?"

2. By then, Cousin Phoebe had her answer, which she gave him. She then counterattacked, saying, "If I bet that you couldn't make an egg spin for more than ten seconds before it stopped, what kind of egg would you want? Raw or hard boiled?" Theo started to answer, but my Cousin Phoebe fixed him with a devastating look. "And furthermore," she said, "why?"

3. Theo managed to field that one, and he came straight back with a stunner. "If you had a glass of water filled to the brim, how many toothpicks, if any, could you put in the glass without spilling any water?"

   "I wouldn't know until I tried," she said. "And neither would you."

   "Well, *about* how many?" Theo said, persisting. "About two or three, or fifty or more?"

4. My Cousin Phoebe answered and then countered with one that she must have read recently because, as I said, she ain't no scientist. "If you were a diamond miner and were paid by weight, where would you prefer to have your diamonds weighed? At the bottom of the mine, or at the top?"

5. Theo was a little shaky by now and he looked worried, but he gave his answer and then said, "If you and me were carrying a heavy couch up a flight of stairs, which end would you rather take?"

6. "You and I," my Cousin Phoebe said, before supplying the answer. "Better watch your grammar, Theo. And now let's see how observant you are. You've looked at your watch and all the clocks in your house hundreds of times. Tell me, which is longer, the second hand or the minute hand, or are they both the same?"

   Theo started to sneak a look at his wristwatch, but his mother smiled sweetly and said, "Now, Theo, don't cheat." "Who's cheating—I'm not cheating," Theo said in a fury. "Besides, it's a stupid question and I don't have to answer it."

   Needless to say, my Cousin Phoebe was never invited to one of Theo's birthday parties again.

*Solution on page 57.*

# BY APPOINTMENT ONLY

$A$t its headquarters in a New York suburb, Hubbec International, which derives its name from the days when it made hubs near a small beck in rural New York, rules the world of plastic reproductions of wild animals. Today, its luxurious offices house one of the finest collections of French nineteenth-century painting and ceramics in the world. The various items of the collection are kept in the offices of Hubbec executives, and twice a year the works can be seen by a select few who are shown around in groups of six.

My Cousin Phoebe was among these elite. In her excitement to see one of her favorite Cezannes, she arrived early and was the first of her group to be ushered into a salon used as a waiting room. On entering, she saw what you see. After a moment or two, she rushed out to give her news to the attendant who had brought her in. What did my Cousin Phoebe see, and what did she tell the attendant?

---

## Questions

1. Do you think that security was slack at Hubbec Headquarters?

2. Do you think the room was furnished by a professional decorator?

3. Would a professional decorator place a vase where it obstructed a section of a painting?

4. What did my Cousin Phoebe notice, and what do you think she should have done about it?

*Solution on page 58.*

# THE END OF EUPHORIA

$E$verybody in the town of Columbo regarded Dizzy McNish not only as slow-witted, but as one of the most incompetent police officers in the state, and yet—

He was driving along Route 2½ and thinking of Marcella McNish and all the little Mc-Nishes when he spotted a car parked on Weepers Lane, just off the highway. He turned in to investigate, and he saw what you see here. The body was still warm, and after identifying the victim as Euphoria Gotcha, McNish called the State Criminal Investigation Bureau.

Since this was McNish's jurisdiction and he was technically in charge, the state investigators told him that this was the seventh of the hitchhiker killings, all with bodies found in the same position and with the same modus operandi. In the other six cases, the murders had not been discovered until a day or two after their commission, but this time the trail was fresh and there were more clues. Having given McNish the pertinent information, the state investigators suggested politely that he get lost.

Stung to the quick by this high-handed treatment and anxious to be a hero to the littlest of the McNishes (Allegra, age 6), McNish wandered around Columbo and arrested every person he didn't know by name. He managed to find three, pictured here and identified by name.

McNish looked them up and down carefully, very carefully. Then he scratched his head (he had dandruff) and realized he had ample proof for an accusation. The murder charge stuck and everybody in Columbo was dumbfounded, except of course Marcella and Allegra.

Can you, by examining the scene and studying the three suspects, reconstruct the crime and point out the perpetrator?

---

## Questions

1. Was robbery the apparent motive for the killing?

2. Did the perpetrator sit next to Euphoria?

3. Did the book belong to Euphoria?

4. Was the book essential to the commission of the crime?

5. Was the blow delivered with the left hand?

6. Did the slacks belong to the perpetrator?

7. Was the perpetrator a woman?

8. Did the perpetrator leave in a hurry?

9. Which of the three suspects killed Euphoria?

10. Can you reconstruct the crime?

*Solution on page 59.*

# THE THREE GRACES

F̲ew of those who were invited to the Nineties' benefit affair, held on the estate of the Baroness Calvados-Slivovitz, had ever heard of either akrokanthera or of Hector Moneylove, so let me explain.

Both are poison. Akrokanthera is an African arrow poison that acts almost instantly, and Hector Moneylove is a more subtle form and comes from Chicago. Hector is (or was) a large, handsome man who kicked dogs, slapped children, and robbed their piggy banks whenever he had the chance. That, however, was a mere hobby, and his true vocation was gypping widows and orphans of their inheritances. Several of his victims had been reduced to committing suicide.

Among those who had survived, however, were the Three Graces—the graces respectively of youth, maturity, and old age. It was certainly no coincidence that they met with Hector at the baroness's party, flirted outrageously, plied him with the special Slivovitz distilled from the baroness's own sloes, and then left him stretched out on what became his deathbed.

Sketch A is the replica of a photograph taken by one of the guests at the party. Sketch B shows the Three Graces a few minutes later when they were among those questioned concerning Hector's death. Shortly afterwards, all were released for lack of evidence, but when the autopsy showed that death had resulted from a needlelike puncture in which akrokanthera had been injected, the trio was questioned again. Each of the three said she could have obtained a vial of the poison, but hadn't.

On the basis of the facts above, who do you think killed Hector?

---

## Questions

1. Did each of the Three Graces have a motive for killing Hector?

2. Do you think they deliberately set out to get Hector drunk?

3. Do you think that they planned the murder in advance?

4. Who had the physical opportunity of injecting or applying the akrokanthera?

5. Who do you think killed Hector?

*Solution on page 60.*

# THE VANDALS

Libby Forsyte would have graced the White House and won the war on drugs, solved the education crisis, and balanced the federal budget . . . if she'd been president. But she wasn't. Instead, she exercised her political talents in the small town of Bicrickety, population unknown. In the course of her work on various committees for town betterment, she made many friends *and* many enemies. One of the latter came out of the bushes one lovely October evening and slugged her just as she reached her door. She managed to stagger inside and reach the telephone before she fainted.

Luckily she had no serious injuries, and the next day she was able to attend a police lineup. Chief Earl Hawk had rounded up four suspects who had no alibis for the previous evening and were known to have threatened Libby as a "Do Gooder." But before going to headquarters, Libby asked her young friend, my Cousin Phoebe, to examine the scene of the assault and then go with her to the lineup.

The scene of the crime is sketched here, plus the four suspects. They are, from top to bottom, Tom Foolery, an irresponsible TV mechanic; James Patrick Parker III, a fashion plate; Ike the Pike, a gas station attendant; and Everett Zoot, who had no apparent means of support, and shaved only once every two weeks.

At first, Libby was unable to point out her assailant, but my Cousin Phoebe whispered something in her ear, after which Libby brightened up and made a positive identification, which subsequently held up in court. When my Cousin Phoebe was asked how she'd been able to identify the culprit, she answered tersely.

"Common sense," she said. "Just examine the door and then take a look at these four. That's how."

By studying the room and the message scrawled on the sliding door, can you point out the perpetrator?

---

## Questions

1. Was the attack on Libby malicious?

2. Had the perpetrator planned ahead of time to write his message?

3. How did he write his message? With a paintbrush? With his fingers? With the rags?

4. How did the blotches occur?

5. Who slugged Libby and committed the acts of vandalism.

*Solution on page 60.*

# 57TH HEAVEN

Pokey Pokenose took pictures of everything and everybody he saw, whether they liked it or not. He had photos of his parents, of his friends, and of his two sisters—snapped when they weren't looking. Naturally, when he'd been ordered to stay away from Joe Lugnut's garage, he sneaked in one morning at 10 A.M. and took the picture shown in sketch A. When he heard a noise, he got scared and ran away.

About 4 P.M. he returned and took the picture shown in sketch B. After comparing it with A, he called the police.

What did the police do, and what did they say to Pokey?

A

## Questions

1. Had Joe Lugnut, the man under the car, moved between 10 A.M. and 4 P.M.?

2. Had the hand holding the wrench moved?

3. Was Lugnut killed before or after Pokey took photo A?

4. What did the police infer when they entered the garage?

5. What did the police say to Pokey?

6. What were the ten differences that the police noted in the two sketches, and what action did they take as a result?

*Solution on page 61.*

B

# Bombs in Toyland

Martin Sloppentropper, owner of Sloppentropper's department store, had been having labor trouble. Early on the morning in which his Christmas display was due to open (October, of course), he received a phone call warning him that a bomb had been planted in the toy department. He immediately notified the police, who were in the store when Sloppentropper arrived and saw what you see.

The bomb, which had been placed on the sled in the Blue Grotto (arrow indicates where), had already been removed by the police. They were looking for clues when Sloppentropper showed up.

"Everything is supposed to be blue," he said to the toy buyer. "Who put that green blanket on the sled?"

The toy buyer pointed to the merchandise on the other side of the aisle. "It came from there," he said. "Whoever took it had the choice of any color he wanted—red, blue, green— they're all there."

Sloppentropper said "Ah!" and had no further ideas, but the police continued with their work. First, they narrowed the investigation down to four suspects—the decorator who had designed the exhibit, the carpenter and electrician who had worked on the grotto last night, and the night watchman.

The decorator, electrician, and carpenter each said he'd been the first to leave. The police were left wondering who had planted the bomb and then turned off the bright lights required for their work.

The watchman was no help. He said he'd been on the midnight to 8 A.M. shift, that he'd made his regular rounds, and that when he'd arrived the store had been dark except for the dim nightlights, so dim that he had to use his flashlight.

The police were stymied until my Cousin Phoebe came along. She'd been wandering around the store and, after seeing the crowd clustered at the Blue Grotto exhibit, asked a few questions, examined the sled, and acquired the information you have, on the basis of which she told the police who had planted the bomb.

Whom did she accuse, and why?

---

## Questions

1. Is there any reason to believe the alibis of
   (a) the decorator?
   (b) the electrician?
   (c) the carpenter?

2. Is the watchman's statement credible?

3. Do you think that the dropcloth was accidentally torn by the bomber in the course of placing the bomb?

4. Do you think that the green blanket was selected in order to differentiate it from the blue objects?

5. Do you think that the green blanket was placed on the sled before midnight?

6. Who planted the bomb?

*Solution on page 62.*

# THE THREE WISE MEN

Winkle, Blinkle, and Knott were drowsing in the Marlborough Room of the exclusive Club 23½ and swore that nobody had gone past them and into the library during the two hours they'd been snoozing. Furthermore, none of them had stirred except Winkle, to get a magazine, Blinkle to order drinks, and Knott to put another log on the fire. Nevertheless, Rosco Mailer, the club steward (better known as "Blackie"), was found in the adjacent library, quite dead from the combination of a blow and the impact of his skull on the marble floor.

It was Stinky Walters, son of the club bartender, who found the body. He admitted he'd snuck past the trio on his way to the library, where he hoped to find an illustrated copy of the *Arabian Nights*. But instead of Aladdin and Sinbad, he found the body of Blackie, who was hated by many and loved by none. He had managed to keep his job because he'd bugged some of the club bedrooms and had enough on various members, including the trio in the library, to give him the monthly stipend which he considered adequate to his station in life.

Stinky's rather exuberant yell practically popped Winkle, Blinkle, and Knott out of their chairs. They came tottering into the library and stared at the corpse. Then, touching nothing, they called the police.

Chief Prantz responded with enthusiasm, as if he'd been elected to the club itself, but, with nobody to arrest, he got lost in the vacuum of his own thinking. Stinky? Too young, just fourteen years old. And the trio in the library? Too old, in their seventies and eighties. Which left nobody to charge except Donnigan, the waiter who'd brought the drinks, but what evidence was there against him?

That was the situation when my Cousin Phoebe came to drive her uncle Blinkle home. Coming into the room and realizing that everybody was confused and that Chief Prantz was now a little sorry he'd come, she asked what had happened. It was reconstructed as shown. It took her less than five minutes to size up the situation and put Prantz out of his misery.

What did my Cousin Phoebe see, and whom did she tell Prantz to accuse?

---

## Questions

1. Do Chief Prantz's reasons for eliminating the first four suspects make sense?

2. Do you think that the murderer brought his weapon with him and still had it when he left?

3. Who killed Blackie?

*Solution on page 62.*

# At the Professional Level

$B$y now, you've had considerable experience in crime solving. Your wits have been sharpened and your powers of observation have been polished to a high gloss. So now let's see how you stack up against a trained detective.

The accompanying sketches were reproduced from Professor James Osterburg's book, *The Crime Laboratory*\*, which he uses in his classes in criminal investigation at the University of Illinois. These case studies are designed to test his students' ability to compare microphotographs of two objects, such as fingerprints or bullets or individual letters of two typewriters.

Professor Osterburg suggests that you number each area of examination in a gridiron pattern and then compare it with the same area of the second sketch. If in your comparison you can spot all the differences within five minutes, you deserve an A in Osterburg's class. My Cousin Phoebe got a perfect score in two minutes flat. As for myself—don't ask.

So—how many differences can *you* find?

\*Copyright © 1982 by Clark Boardman Company, Ltd., 375 Hudson Street, New York, NY 10014. Reprinted by permission of Clark Boardman Company, Ltd., from *The Crime Laboratory*, pages 129, 207, 394.

*Solution on page 63.*

On the day that Battling Bimbow moved into his rental house on Windless Beach, he announced that he hated dogs and intended to get rid of any that trespassed on his property. By the seventh day, three of his neighbors were bereft of their pets. On the eighth day Bimbow himself was found dead, but there was this difference: Fido, Rover, and Spot died of poison, whereas Bimbow succumbed to a hammer—wielded fatally, efficiently, and with malice aforethought.

The police investigation narrowed the field down to four suspects. They were:

Brenda Bimbow, wife, who claimed she'd gone to the city on a shopping expedition, although she'd bought nothing;

Sidney Slide, who claimed he'd been home reading Proust;

Rita Bargos, who said she'd been in her own home all day long while conducting a memorial service for Fido;

Jenny Penn, who said she'd been writing a novel.

After removing the body, the police searched the rest of the house for clues. They were getting nowhere until my Cousin Phoebe, searching for driftwood on the beach, saw the police and walked into the house. After seeing what you see and realizing that Chief Aristide Buttonwiggs was stumped, she took him aside and made a suggestion, as a result of which he made an arrest.

What did she suggest, and what did Buttonwiggs do about it?

## Questions

1. Had the room been cleaned lately?

2. Why do you think the chairs were on top of the table and the big chair upended?

3. Did the perpetrator leave in a hurry?

4. On the basis of the answers to the last three questions, what important clue or clues do you now have?

5. What do you think my Cousin Phoebe suggested to Chief Buttonwiggs?

*Solution on page 63.*

# THE MARCH OF THE MARCHIONESS

My Cousin Phoebe was at the other side of the Café Discrète when the Marchioness of Secks-Ruma came in screaming. Later everybody agreed that she'd hit a high C and kept it there, which is an accomplishment even for a marchioness. Furthermore, one of the couples along her line of march heard her say, under her breath, "I bet the wily lout took it."

Despite the general confusion, however, my Cousin Phoebe managed to calm her down and extract a coherent account of what had set her off. She said she'd been having a drink with Bobo Bolingbrook, with whom she had been accused of having an affair. She denied it vehemently, stating that they were merely a couple of old friends reminiscing over a drink, in the course of which she took off her $100,000 necklace to show him. She said it was lying on the table when she suddenly remembered she had an appointment with Percy Peashooter, her hairdresser. At the realization, she jumped up and accidentally bumped into a waiter, knocking over his tray. Embarrassed, she rushed out but only got as far as the lobby when, according to her account, she realized she'd left her necklace on the table, whereupon she dashed back to find no necklace and no sign of Bobo.

"Oh my necklace!" she exclaimed. "Bobo, how could you do such a thing!"

My Cousin Phoebe listened carefully to every word, studied the table and the mess on the floor, after which she took the marchioness aside and told the management not to worry, she'd handle it.

What did she say to the marchioness, and what did the marchioness do?

## Questions

1. Did the marchioness leave abruptly?

2. Did Bobo rush out after her?

3. Do you think Bobo picked up the necklace and walked off with it?

4. Do you believe that Bobo and the marchioness could have conspired to make up a story that would explain the disappearance of the necklace, subsequently to be claimed as an insurance loss?

5. Do marchionesses usually mutter under their breath with sufficient clarity to be overheard as they pass a table?

6. What do you think my Cousin Phoebe told the marchioness?

*Solution on page 64.*

# SOLUTIONS

## Solution to *Introduction* (p. vii)

There are six F's in this sentence. If you guessed lower, don't despair—most people only count three or four the first time through. Go back again and count carefully.

## Solution to *A Tale of Hate* (p. 1)

1. No. They are all too common in the Southern California desert.

2. Yes. She'd been wearing high leather boots, even though she was dressed for warm weather.

3. No. Normally they attack only when disturbed or threatened.

4. Yes, with the exception of the boots and the gunny sack in the closet, everything is scrupulously neat.

5. Yes, since the light is on.

6. No, because if it had been, she would have seen her dress and probably gone directly to it before taking off her boots. It follows that she must have opened the closet door.

7. It must have been brought in, probably in the gunny sack.

8. It must have been in the closet, because with the room well lit she would have seen the snake, particularly because she was always aware that Hector was planning to kill her. Furthermore, she would not have taken off her boots until she felt she was safe from any eventuality.

9. She must have been startled and frightened by the snake, which apparently attacked her when she opened the closet door.

10. Since Hector left in daylight, it must have been Salvina who turned on the lights when she entered the house. She then took off her boots, saw Hector's note, and, anxious to see her new dress, opened the closet door. The snake, startled by the sudden light and the appearance of a large body, attacked, biting Salvina on the leg. With the phone inoperable because Hector must have pulled it from its socket, she lay there helplessly until the wandering minstrel arrived.

    Realizing the nature of the emergency, the minstrel killed the snake, located and administered anti-snake serum, hooked up the phone, and called for help.

As a result of his quick actions, the minstrel saved Salvina's life and she regarded him forever as a hero. Her hate turned to love and they were married. After which, he wandered no more.

## Solution to *Board to Death* (p. 3)

1. No, because the directors have already taken notes, probably on some other matter.

2. Yes. The knife penetrated to the hilt.

3. Yes, because knives are not usually supplied at board meetings, and therefore the killer must have brought the knife with him.

4. Yes. We know that the murder was planned ahead of time, and there is no apparent way the killer could have been sitting in the room and triggered a short circuit without being noticed.

5. Yes. It takes about fourteen seconds for the average person to adjust his vision from light to dark or vice versa. There-fore, the killer had to time his attack while everyone in the room was temporarily blind, including himself.

6. Either Funny Fonson or Dodo Dodson, since they were closest to him.

7. Funny Fonson. The angle of the knife from left to right and delivered from behind the victim would be natural for a left-hander but would be extremely awkward for a right-hander, especially if he was in a hurry. The placement of Funny Fonson's glass, plus the slant of his writing, point conclusively to him as a lefty.

Faced with the evidence, Fonson asked, "Can I at least have those new pajamas while I'm in prison?"

Request denied.

## Solution to *A Pair of Roos* (p. 5)

Micklemouse answered thusly: "The two kangaroos would arrive at exactly the same instant, because each of them would be moving at the velocity of the earth, plus their own speeds, which are identical.

"To illustrate," he continued, "suppose you're standing at the exact center of a railroad car that's traveling at seventy miles an hour. At each end of the car and at the same distance from you, you're offered a martini, one with an olive, the other with a twist of lemon. No matter how much you love martinis and in which direction you go, provided you walk at the same pace and don't fall on your face, you will get your martini at the same moment. Same goes for a drink of water, although your pace may be slower. And whether the train is going from New York to Los Angeles or vice versa is irrelevant."

"Thank you, I just wanted to make sure," the hoary stranger said, and vanished.

# Solution to *The Fair Evangeline* (p. 7)

1. No. His bare word is unsupported.

2. No. Like the Admirable Farragut, C. Starr's bare word is unsupported.

3. No, although the approximate time when the painting was made could be ascertained by the position of the moon on the relevant night.

4. Yes. He might have killed the Fair Evangeline in the course of a lover's quarrel.

5. Yes. He might have killed his wife because he thought her unfaithful.

6. At the grave site, because a path of reflected light travels from the source (in this case the moon) to the eye of the observer. Therefore, Farragut stood at the grave site, and not near the ruined house, which he stated was a mile away.

7. Farragut, because, as proved by the answer to question 6, he lied, and the painting is proof of the lie. On the basis of the painting, the jury had no trouble convicting him of murder.
   "I admit I made a mistake," he said, "but at least my reputation as an artist is unquestioned."
   On that, the jury took no stand.

---

# Solution to *Whiz Kid* (p. 9)

1. At the very least, she knew the phone number, which she tried to tell her father ("You can phone me at—"). Probably the kidnappers had mentioned it without realizing they were overheard.

2. Yes. She scribbled her own name several times, as kids often do.

3. Probably. This would certainly be consistent with Sally's character.

4. Yes, otherwise they would have destroyed the bit of paper, rather than throwing it away.

5. Yes, in which case they would have found out that the number was fictitious and of no importance.

6. A telephone dial. As a child she had probably been using telephones almost since infancy, and being unusually bright, she could easily visualize the telephone dial.

7. It gave the street address, which you can figure out.
   In case you need a hint, you merely substitute each number with one of the three letters on the corresponding button of your phone dial. Since the numeral (1) has no accompanying letters, it is either a numeral or is being used as a blank space to separate numbers from letters.
   The police, using the above reasoning, figured out that the address was 7293 Maple, where they found Sally

expecting them. By midnight, the kidnappers were in police custody and she was home and safe.

She was jubilant at being rescued, but disappointed at learning that the police rather than her parents had figured things out.

"I still love you," she told them, "but I thought you were a lot brighter than the police."

## Solution to *Witness, the Cat* (p. 11)

1. Yes.

2. No likely place is visible, and hiding it in the room would have been unbelievably stupid.

3. Probably not, because the excision is clean and required a steady hand. A drunk would have botched the job.

4. No. No one outside the room could have slid the bolt from its seating and then slid it back, and the treetops show that the room is on an upper floor which could not have been reached without a ladder.

5. Dilly obviously stood on its hind legs and propped itself on its fore-paws, which is no way for a cat to go to the bathroom. Besides, cats do a thorough job of cleaning up after their own mess, and the earth is only slightly ruffled. There is no indication of anything to eat on the bon-kei tray, but the empty pool could be evidence that the cat may have lapped up whatever liquid was in it.

6. Judging by the trail of paw prints, it must have lost its balance as it tried to climb onto the mantle. The cat appears to be drunk, apparently from lapping at the bon-kei pool.

7. Anthony Adipose, who was only pretending to be drunk (note that the chips and cards in front of him are still neat). As the one nearest to the bon-kei, it appears he had been dumping liquor into the bon-kei, thus soaking the earth and filling the pool. A police search led to Adipose's apartment, where they found his thin wife gazing rapturously at the Renoir. With all the notoriety surrounding the theft, experts questioned the provenance of the painting and declared it a fake. The club then expelled Adipose and replaced the supposed Renoir with a Rose Treat seaweed collage.

# Solution to *Involving the Rear End* (p. 13)

1. A good question. He probably was, but it is difficult to give a clear answer.

2. Yes. He was flying a kite.

3. No.

4. Yes. Dogs are territorial and usually defend their territory, as they conceive it to be.

5. No, because the dog came from the direction from which the wind was blowing (note the angle of the kite string, and the position of the birds, who face into the oncoming wind). The wind could therefore not have carried Nutty's scent in the dog's direction.

6. It seems that the distant figure, Sykes's, would be able to see Nutty. But even if he couldn't, he would see the kite flying above, and would probably decide that the man on the other end of the string was his long-standing enemy, Nutty Fregosa.

7. Against Sykes, the defendant. Since the dog could not have scented Nutty, and since Sykes had probably seen him or his kite, it follows that the dog attacked because he was ordered to. The only question then was how much Nutty should collect. The judge assessed the damages at $1000.

   Nutty was jubilant. "One grand," he said, "and Sissy, too!"

---

# Solution to *Play On, Oh Lovely Music* (p. 15)

1. All three musicians, as well as Miss Turner, probably had equal opportunities.

2. His own picture, nude.

3. No.

4. Because he was not only surprised and shocked, but enraged at the attack on his dignity.

5. Little Miss Turner, since she was clearly waiting to see how he would react, and therefore must have known what he would see when he turned the page.

   Although she could hardly have anticipated what followed, she never had any regrets. She is now happily married and lives in a small town where she plays the church organ every Sunday. She has maintained her friendship with the surviving members of the quartet, and she visits the prison regularly and acts as a courier between Evelina and the two string players.

   Paige's husband is a journalist and gave the story of the Quirkenbocker group considerable publicity. As a result, he was able to persuade a TV producer to give the trio a TV contract, when and if they are released from prison.

   All three musicians are enthusiastic and anxious to form their own trio, although Evelina has stipulated that she be given a new page turner, since she says that the presence of Paige would evoke memories that are best forgotten.

"Forgotten?" the former little Miss Turner said. "But Gaston simply loved being in the nude, and I should know because—" And she hesitated and smiled prettily.

---

## Solution to *Without Mirrors, Please* (p. 17)

1. Will reads as follows:

   *I, Roger Honiger Shrew, of the town of Shrewville, N.Y., do hereby make this my last will and testament.*

   *Since all my next of kin, with the exception of the nephew named below, are rotten to the core and unworthy of being my heirs, I therefore give and bequeath everything that I possess to my nephew Hans Muller.*

   *Signed and dated this Thanksgiving Day of November 17, 1988.*

2. No. April 1 is as valid a date as any other in the calendar. Characterizing the day has no legal force whatsoever.

3. The sheet of carbon paper must have been put face up over another sheet, and then the original was written. Without that middle sheet between the carbon and the original, the mirror writing would have been on the back of the top sheet.

4. It is suspect because Thanksgiving Day is always on the fourth Thursday of November, which November 17 could not possibly be. Hans, a foreigner who was not even in the United States on the seventeenth, made a mistake that no American was likely to make, particularly when writing a document as important as a will.

   The carbon reproduced here was therefore open to the suspicion of forgery and the suspicion was confirmed by a group of handwriting experts. They reasoned that Hans had probably used the carbon device purposely, because it blurred the lettering and made it more difficult to analyze.

   The three nephews were jubilant as they watched Hans bundled off to jail. Then, realizing their narrow escape from losing everything, they decided to split the fortune three ways and drink a toast to Roger Honiger and his frustrated scheme to make them quarrel.

   And they lived happily ever after.

---

## Solution to *Tale of a Tub* (p. 19)

1. Yes, but with some difficulty.

2. Yes. According to reports, he was barely over five feet tall.

3. Yes. He had lost out to Alphonso in the bidding, and the idea of a Brazilian sitting in the sacred tub that Napoleon had once used would be anathema to any true Frenchman.

4. Yes. The tub could not possibly have

54

been Napoleon's camping tub because the circular patches at one end of the tub show where faucets had once been. Even if Napoleon had running water in his palaces, he certainly didn't have it on the battlefield. His valets poured hot water from pitchers until the tub was full. It follows that this tub was a fake. The fixture marks must have been painted over, but emerged clearly after Alphonso's frequent use.

5. Yes. Since it will probably eventually be revealed that her tub is a fake, she is wide open to a suit for the return of $50,000.

6. Not likely, but who knows? Tastes hide in many corners.

7. There is no evidence of a struggle here, although it seems incredible that Alphonso sat peacefully in his tub and submitted to an attack.

8. Marshal Nay, who gave point to the adage that no man is a hero to his valet. He made the mistake of admitting he was in the house, and so would certainly have known who was the last person to have visited Alphonso and whether it was a man or a woman. Therefore, he must have lied, perhaps because he was afraid of being questioned on details. But what clinched his guilt was the fact that the bathroom was spotlessly clean. Any blood, and there must have been some, any evidence of violence, and again there must have been some, had been cleaned up. A towel hung on the rack and a spotless bath mat was set down next to the tub. Obviously neither Roland nor Josephine would bother to tidy up, but a valet, trained to do so, would, could, and did.

"I never could stand a mess," Nay said.

The moral is, don't be too tidy. It can incriminate you.

## Solution to *Spitfire* (p. 21)

1. Yes.

2. Yes, witness the deserted mower and the partly cut grass.

3. No. The fact that he'd made passes at her before, and her comment to her friend would suggest she would never have had a drink with him.

4. Yes, quite possibly. In the course of divorce proceedings, there are often moments of regret and friendship.

5. None of them. Jesse would hardly sit quietly and watch somebody ruin her liquor cabinet.

6. No. The note is in handwriting that differs from the other notes on the refrigerator, proving that it was not written by Jesse. As for Nick, he never would have written a note that would incriminate him.

7. No. Judging by the amount of wine in the two glasses and the amount left in the recently opened bottle, it seems evident that nobody drank any wine that morning. Instead, we have evi-

dence of a frame-up. After killing Jesse, the murderer must have broken open the cabinet, taken and opened a bottle of wine, and poured some of it into two glasses.

8. Angel. We not only have eliminated Nicholas, but the existence of a frame-up points to someone experienced in crime and trickery, and Sweet William had neither the experience nor the brains to commit a crime as sophisticated as this one. Add it all up, and Felicity had no trouble making up her mind.

Shortly before her trial, Angel Blackhead made the following statement: "Shows what happens to people who go trespassing. Me, I would never do such a thing. I live by the law and die by the law."

The jury carried out his wishes.

---

## Solution to *All Around the Maypole* (p. 23)

1. Yes, because no one else was near her.

2. Yes, in a bouquet of flowers.

3. No. They were concentrating on their dancing, and in the confusion of falling they would be unlikely to notice anything or anyone else. Try falling down with a few of your friends, but decorously and without breaking bones, and see how little you notice.

4. Yes. Bub apparently watched for some time before deciding to attack, and he must have had some reason, such as a signal, to go into action.

5. (b) A dancer, because with the crowd behind Bub, only the dancers were in his view.

6. Yes, because of the answer to question 5, and because the perpetrator must have brought the knife with her.

7. Belinda, because she was in line directly behind Cherie and could point to her without calling attention to the gesture, and because Belinda was in the best position to attack. Dearie, in front of Cherie, would have had to turn around to signal. This would have been difficult for any of the other dancers to do without being observed.

8. Belinda, as indicated above. Poor gal, it turned out that she was jealous of Cherie, but needn't have been. Leo the Lecher, the guy Belinda was after, wasn't really serious about Cherie. He said he was just trying her out for size, and the same went for Belinda, whom he wooed for a day or two, and left. He ended up picking Ecstata, but she turned him down as too dangerous.

Served him right, too.

# Solution to *Ex Libris* (p. 25)

1. No, there was no sign of it.

2. To conceal the sound of the shot and cause a general commotion.

3. Yes. They were torn out of his notebook.

4. Robbery, as evidenced by the fact that pages were taken from Pinchnose's notebook.

5. No. Sammy is hardly the intellectual type.

6. There is no evidence to prove or to disprove his account, but he had no reason to set off the alarm and therefore his story is credible.

7. Goody, who as librarian had access to and familiarity with all parts of the library, including closets.

8. Goody. Her statement that she knew Pinchnose was writing a book, and writing it about the Venerable Bede is suspicious. In view of the possibility that she might be writing a book on the same subject and was afraid someone would publish it before her, you have her motive. Furthermore, only she and Sammy knew of the existence and whereabouts of the alarm clock. But the final item that enabled my Cousin Phoebe to solve the case was the fact that the librarian is the proverbial "invisible man," unnoticed because he or she is part of the *entourage*. Anyone else would not only have been noticed, but remembered.

   Arrested and charged, Goody asked for solitary confinement so that she could write her book without further interruption.

---

# Solution to *A Matter of Gravity* (p. 27)

1. No. The bale of furs would weigh less at the equator because the speed of the surface of the equator is faster (it has further to go at each revolution). Therefore, objects tend to be thrown outward with greater force than at the poles, thus to a slight extent countering the force of gravity.

   The great speed at the equator tends to create a slight bulge on the earth, so that an object on the equator is further from the center of the earth than an object at the pole, where the earth is slightly flattened. Consequently, the pull of gravity is stronger at the pole—but don't try to measure it.

2. Hard boiled. It would spin longer because it is a solid. Consequently, all of its bulk is pulled equally to the earth by gravity; whereas the raw egg is a liquid that sloshes around, thus pulling or pushing the egg in various directions and weakening the effect of gravity.

3. Fifty or more, because the surface tension of the water creates a slight bulge, on the surface of which quite a few toothpicks would rest. The toothpicks would not be floating *in* the water, but resting on top of it and not displacing any of the liquid.

4. At the top, where the diamonds would be slightly heavier because gravity would be stronger there. Gravity is the pull of all objects to each other in a kind of mutual attraction. At the bottom of the mine, some of the earth's pull would be acting above the diamond and pulling it up, so that the net force would be lessened.

5. The higher end. The man at the lower end would have the heavier burden because he is closer to the couch's center of gravity. You can test this by taking a plank and holding it first at one end, then halfway to the center, then close to the center. Tilting the plank shifts the weight toward the lower end.

6. The second hand is longer. Although it appears to be the same length as the minute hand, the second hand is longer because of the short extension that protrudes beyond the center point of the dial.

## Solution to *By Appointment Only* (p. 29)

1. Yes, because my Cousin Phoebe was left alone in a room where she could have easily stolen anything portable.

2. Yes, because everything matches, including drapes, and the perfection and balance of the room cry out its professionalism.

3. No, this would be contrary to his or her training.

4. She noticed that the bridal vase had probably been moved from the end of the mantel, where there is a slight stain. She also reasoned that, where there's a bride, there should be a groom; therefore the groom vase must have been stolen, due to the same poor security that left her alone in the room. On the chance that the thief was still in the building and still had the vase, my Cousin Phoebe pulled the alarm.

Naturally, it turned out that she had guessed right, and the thief was apprehended at the front door.

In a fine show of gratitude for what she'd done, one of the top Hubbec officials thanked my Cousin Phoebe personally and gave her a plastic reproduction of a puma.

My Cousin Phoebe gave it to the first small child she happened to see. At the next art showing at Hubbec six months later, she ran into the same executive. He greeted her by saying, "How's your puma?"

My Cousin Phoebe blushed.

# Solution to *The End of Euphoria* (p. 31)

1. Yes, judging by the open pocketbook.

2. Yes, because the rear of the car was crammed with baggage. No one would let an unknown hitchhiker sit in back when the front passenger seat was available.

3. No. It is unlikely that Euphoria would turn off the road to examine her own book, and then become so interested in it that she was unaware of the actions of the passenger who sat beside her. But if she was shown the mystery book, she probably became too absorbed to notice the rest of the world.

4. Yes. Only if Euphoria was bending forward and concentrating on the book would the perpetrator have had the chance to stab Euphoria in the back without resistance.

5. Yes. To stab Euphoria in the back with the right hand would be impossible without interrupting her reading. Poor thing, she was a sucker for a whodunit.

6. Yes, because they were bloodstained.

7. Yes, judging by the discarded slacks, which button on the side and have no fly.

8. Yes, because in this case important evidence, such as the knife and the book, were left behind. In earlier cases, the perpetrator had plenty of time to remove any incriminating evidence.

9. Ittle Bopeek. First, because we know that the perpetrator was a woman; second, because the broken end of a shoelace, complete with aglet, lies on the floor of the car and matches the short end of the lace of Ittle's left shoe. McNish was certain that of his three suspects, Ittle was the murderer.

10. While there may be other reasonable theories, the evidence strongly suggests that Ittle asked Euphoria to drop her off on Weepers Lane. When she stopped, Ittle, before getting out, handed Euphoria the book. Euphoria became so absorbed in the whodunit that Ittle found it easy to take out her knife and stab Euphoria in the back. After that, Ittle emptied the pocketbook and pushed the seat back to give herself plenty of room to undress. She then took off her shoes and her bloodstained slacks, exchanging them for the pair on the hanger holding the suit.

    From what Ittle admitted in her rambling account to the police, whenever she needed money, voices told her exactly how to get it. As Euphoria stopped for her, the voices came loud and clear, and she obeyed them as she always had. She had completed the crime and was putting on her shoes when she heard somebody coming, perhaps McNish. Panicking, she yanked too hard on her shoelace and broke it. Still in a hurry, she tied it up as best she could and ran, abandoning the knife and mystery novel. She felt no remorse, and she had only one regret.

    "I only got halfway through that book myself," she said. "I never did find out who did it."

## Solution to *The Three Graces* (p. 33)

1. Yes. Hector had robbed each of them.

2. Yes. They hated him and would have approached him only for a hostile purpose, and when his defenses were down.

3. Yes. Nobody merely happens to have a bit of akrokanthera around when he or she goes to a lawn party.

4. All three. Each was wearing a hat pin that could have been dipped in the poison. Hector was apparently in no condition to notice what his three charmers did.

5. The oldest Grace, with her hat pin, which, judging by a comparison of the two sketches, had been moved and replaced. The other pins are in exactly the same place in both sketches.

   The above facts did not constitute a strong enough case on which to base a formal charge of murder. The District Attorney, however, was a wily fellow, and invited the trio to a champagne lunch the next day. At the top of each place setting, he set a shiny new hat pin. With these props and enough champagne, he hoped to get a confession, but all he got was laughter. After the luncheon, the Three Graces went to the nearest pawn shop to sell their souvenirs. They were offered ten cents for each pin, and they took their thirty cents and put it in the alms box of the nearest church.

   They stopped laughing the next day when all three were arrested and charged with *conspiracy* to commit murder. Eventually, they were tried by a jury, and acquitted.

   Obviously the jury was seduced by their charm, but principally by whose charm? Which of the three? On that point, the jury disagreed.

---

## Solution to *The Vandals* (p. 35)

1. Yes, highly so, as indicated by the threat and the broken glass.

2. Yes, because he brought stove polish and rags.

3. With his fingers. A cloth would have made broader and more irregular marks, and if he'd used a brush, he would have left it together with his other materials.

4. They must have been made by the ball, or lower part of his hand, which dragged irregularly as he moved his finger to write his message. Since the blotches were to the left of the writing, he must have been left-handed. A right-hander would have dragged the back of his hand to the right.

5. Ike the Pike. He is left-handed, as he shows by blowing his nose with his left hand.

   When accused and told why, Ike protested angrily. Libby tried to calm him down. "Let me talk to him alone," she said to the sergeant. "I want him to know that I bear him no grudge."

   After some discussion, the police

sergeant agreed. "I'll give you five minutes," he said, "but be careful. The man is dangerous."

When the time was up, the sergeant entered the room. Ike was on the floor and holding up his arm, as if to protect himself, and a lump on his forehead was just beginning to show.

"Oh, the poor man!" Libby said, oozing with the milk of human kindness. "I feel so sorry for him." And she put a small iron back in her bag.

---

## Solution to *57th Heaven* (p. 37)

1. No, as far as we can see.

2. Yes, the fingers released their tight grip on the wrench.

3. After, since Joe must have still been alive to grasp the wrench tightly. Upon his death, his fingers loosened their grip on the wrench. Since there is hardly any other movement, Joe must have been killed very shortly after photo A was taken.

4. The removal of the Chevy insignia indicated that the car was hot and was being altered for resale elsewhere. Someone must have gotten to Joe before he could finish the job.

5. They told him he was a smart kid and a good photographer, and that he had a great future as a detective ahead of him.

6. a) The vague mark of somebody's feet.
   b) The fingers holding the wrench were relaxed.
   c) The handprint on the windshield.
   d) A truck in the window of the garage door.
   e) The Chevy insignia had fallen off, or was taken off.
   f) The radio antenna had been bent.
   g) A package on the rear shelf of the car had disappeared.
   h) The car door is slightly ajar.
   i) Outside rearview mirror had been snapped off.
   j) Toolbox had been moved

After studying the photographs and noticing the differences, the police concentrated on the hand print on the windshield. They were able to identify the fingerprints of Unlucky Louy, whom they arrested for the eighth time in his career; but this time it was a homicide charge, and it stuck.

The rest of Louy's gang were mowed down in a drug war (the package had been a drug delivery, now hijacked by another gang). Louy went to prison, his life was saved, and he changed his name from Unlucky to Lucky. But when he was finally released for his exemplary good behavior, he held up the first person he saw and was back in jail within twenty-four hours.

Which proves the old adage—what's in a name?

## Solution to *Bombs in Toyland* (p. 39)

1. No. The alibis can be neither substantiated nor proved false.

2. Yes.

3. Yes.

4. No. It calls attention to something amiss, which is the last thing the bomber would want.

5. No, because in the strong light, the difference in color would be obvious.

6. The watchman, because in the poor light of a flashlight or, even worse, in the light of semidarkness, green and blue are indistinguishable. It follows that the watchman tore the dropcloth and then, wishing to conceal the rip, he covered it with a green blanket, mistaking it for blue.

   If you have any doubts, take a blue cloth or shirt and place it next to a green one in semidarkness and see if you can distinguish them.

   If you can, don't read this puzzle.

## Solution to *The Three Wise Men* (p. 41)

1. No. Nobody is either too young or too old to commit a murder, and besides, in a democratic society everybody has or should have an equal opportunity.

2. No. Once he'd killed Blackie, the killer would not only not want to be seen, but certainly wouldn't want to be seen with a weapon.

3. Knott. A careful examination of the fire set shows that the poker is missing and that it is lying in or on the fire. Since Knott is known to have apparently placed a log on the fire, it is clear not only that he did the killing, but how he did it.

   When charged and told that my Cousin Phoebe was responsible for pointing him out, Knott beamed at her, said, "Smart girl," and collapsed.

   The club doctor pronounced him dead of a heart attack.

# Solution to *At the Professional Level* (p. 43)

These are ten differences, pointed out and numbered for clarity.

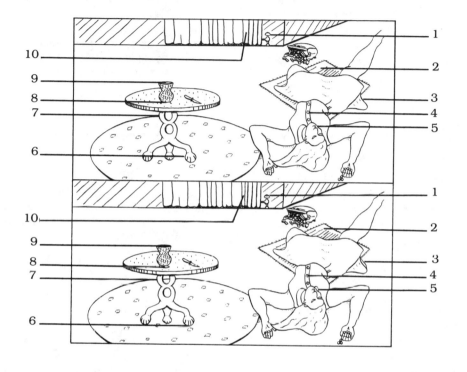

---

# Solution to *Fido, Rover, and Spot* (p. 45)

1. No. The dirty dishes, stuffed ashtray, and crumpled newspaper prove otherwise.

2. In order to vacuum the carpet without obstruction.

3. Yes. He left the chairs on top of the table, and he shoved the vacuum cleaner in the closet without taking the time to make room for it.

4. The vacuum was used a short time ago, and for a specific reason, since the rest of the apartment is untidy. It was then shoved hurriedly into the closet, without time to place it neatly where it was usually stored.

5. She told him to look into the bag of the vacuum cleaner for any possible clues, which he did. He found a number of small green beads, which he decided

must have belonged to the killer and been dropped in the course of committing the crime. The killer, afraid that the beads would prove his or her presence, used the vacuum to pick them up. Under pressure for time, the killer failed to empty the bag.

Once the above facts were established, Buttonwiggs merely had to discover who had or had had a necklace of green beads, and his investigation led him to Rita. Confronted with the evidence, she said, "When I went to see that Bimbow, he laughed at me and kept saying, 'Fido and Rover and Spot. Once they were and now they're not,' and I lost my temper and—" She burst into tears. "I should have known better than to wear that old necklace of mind. Penny wise, pound foolish . . . I should have had those beads restrung."

---

## Solution to *The March of the Marchioness* (p. 47)

1. Yes. She left half of her drink, bumped into a waiter, and knocked over his tray.

2. No. He finished his drink, folded his napkin, and left.

3. No, because he was in plain view of a number of people, some of whom would have seen him pick up the necklace.

4. Yes, it is quite possible, although there is no evidence to support such a theory.

5. Even if you don't know any marchionesses, the answer is probably no. Furthermore, when people mutter under their breath, which is only done in second-rate fiction, their mutterings are, by definition, indistinct. Therefore, the marchioness's remark is suspect, as it is self-serving and presumably a basis on which to accuse Bobo of larceny.

6. My Cousin Phoebe probably said she'd noticed the marchioness had apparently taken her napkin with her, which you don't usually do on your way to the hairdresser, and furthermore she had not brought it back with her. It followed that she'd probably wrapped the necklace in the napkin and stashed it somewhere in the lobby, before returning in the hope that Bobo would be accused of the theft. Faced with my Cousin Phoebe's logic, the marchioness admitted she'd hidden the napkin in the floral exhibit in the lobby.

"A mere prank!" the marchioness said. "How clever of you to have found me out."

The management, delighted to have the matter settled without a scandal, thanked my Cousin Phoebe and offered her drinks on the house, which she invited the marchioness to share with her.

They've been friends ever since.

Kathleen Borowik

Lawrence Treat, the author of many mystery novels and countless short stories, is past president and a former director of the Mystery Writers of America, of which he was one of the founders. He received the Edgar Allan Poe award in 1965 for the Best Short Mystery of the Year, and a second Edgar in 1978 for editing the *Mystery Writers' Handbook*. He was a prize-winner at the Crime Writers' International short story contest held in Stockholm in 1981, and he received a special Edgar Allan Poe award in 1986 for his TV story on the Alfred Hitchcock program. He lives on Martha's Vineyard with his artist wife, Rose. This is his seventh pictorial mystery puzzle book, a form he originated.